DEPRESSION ERA GLASS HANDBOOK & PRICING GUIDE

BY DARLYNE CONWAY

© Copyright 1971 Darlyne Conway

(Photos by Joe A. Gibson)

SBN 912092-41-6

Library of Congress Catalog
Card No. 75-184288

Printed and Published in U. S. A. By

Educator Books, Inc.
DRAWER 32, SAN ANGELO, TEXAS 76901

To

All My Loved Ones

PREFACE

It is needless to say that work was involved in researching and compiling this book; but it is important to me to say that I loved and cherished every minute of it. I have so many to thank for helping and inspiring me to continue. Without their "pushing" and words of encouragement I might have "given up".

I wish to give credit to my Mother, Mrs. Robert Cope, for giving me the idea of writing this book. She has many beautiful pieces of depression glass among other lovely pieces of glassware. She has told me many interesting stories of how she acquired this piece and that piece. She got a lot of them through buying oatmeal and tea. I can remember as a child how exciting it was to reach into a box and draw out a dish, not knowing just what piece it would be - just like Christmas!

Another person I wish to give credit to is John Yount. Without his persistence and encouragement I am not sure I would have ever finished this book. In so doing, I have received many wonderful experiences and blessings.

Many remember the depression era as being just hard and lean years but now some good can come from it by selling their depression glass they have saved or stored these many years. These people may not realize what treasures they have. Some collectors would give their "eye teeth" for them. Search your cupboards and your storerooms and clean up that depression glass either for your sheer enjoyment or for selling. Depression glass collectors are growing by the thousands and it is easy to see why.

It is my fondest hope and desire that this book will be of great assistance to my readers by using it as a guide in collecting or selling.

Adam

ADAM------- Jeannette Glass Co. (1932-1934);

	Pink, Green
Ash Tray	1.75
Bowl - covered	10.50
Bowl - cereal	1.75
Bowl - round 9"	5.50
Bowl - oval 10"	5.50
Bowl - small nappy	2.00
Bowl - large nappy	4.50
Butter Dish with cover	16.50
Candleholders	10.00
Candy Jar with cover	8.00
Cake Plate - 10"	8.50

ADAM

Creamer	3.25
Coaster	1.50
Cup	2.50
Saucer	1.75
Pitcher - 8" cone shaped	13.00
Plate - Pie	1.75
Plate - 9"	3.00
Plate - dinner	4.00
Plate - divided	5.00
Platter - 12"	6.00
Relish Plate - oblong	5.00
Salt & Pepper	7.00
Sherbet	2.50
Sugar	3.00
Salt Dish	5.50
Tumbler - 5" - footed	5.00
Tumbler - 6" - footed	5.50
Tumbler	5.00
Vase	8.00

American Sweetheart

AMERICAN SWEETHEART ---- Macbeth-Evans Glass Co. (1930-1936). Pink, Monax (translucent white), clear; Colbalt blue and True Red - very rare & prices are according to what s e l l e r wants for them.

	Pink	Monax
Bowl - berry	2.00	
Bowl - cereal	2.25	5.25
Bowl - serving	5.50	8.50
Bowl - serving - oval	5.50	8.75
Bowl - soup	4.25	7.25
Bowl - fruit - console		27.50
Butter Dish		18.00
Creamer	3.25	6.00
Cup	2.75	5.25
Saucer	1.75	2.50
Pitcher	17.50	
Plate - dinner 10"	3.00	7.25
Plate - luncheon 9"	2.25	6.50
Plate - salad 8"	1.75	5.50
Plate - bread & butter 6"	1.50	4.00
Plate - 11"	6.50	7.50
Plate - 12"		7.50
Plate - 15½"		17.50
Platter	5.50	9.00
Salt & Pepper	9.00	12.50
Sherbet	2.50	3.25
Sugar	3.25	5.50
Sundae Dish - chrome/clear liner (rare)		12.00
Tumbler - juice	2.50	
Tumbler - 4-4½	3.00	

Anniversary

ANNIVERSARY------- Jeannette Glass Co. (1947-49)

Pink, Clear

Bowl - nappy	1.50
Bowl - cereal	2.00
Bowl - 9"	4.25
Butter Dish/cover	13.50
Cake Plate	6.50
Candy Dish/cover - 3 legged	6.00
Creamer	2.25
Cup	1.75
Saucer	1.50
Plate - pie	1.50
Plate - dinner	2.00
Plate - large	4.00
Relish Dish	3.50
Sherbet	2.50
Wine Glass	2.25

Black Diamond Quilted Sherbet Glass 3.00

Black Milk Glass Serving bowl .12.50

AURORA

Bowl 2.00
Cup & saucer 4.00
Glass 4.00
Plate 2.00
Server. 5.00

Black Milk Glass Celery Dish 7.50

11

Basket

BASKET (Lorain)-------Indiana Glass Co. (1929-1932)

Yellow, Green, Crystal,
Opaque White

Bowl - berry (2 sizes) . . . . 3.50 to 5.50

Bowl - cereal 3.00
Bowl - vegetable - oblong 6.00
Bowl - fruit 5.50
Creamer 5.50
Cup 2.75
    Saucer 1.75

BASKET (Lorain)

Plate - 6" pie 2.75
Plate - salad 3.00
Plate - dinner 4.00
Plate - over 10" - cake 5.25
Platter 5.50
Relish Plate - 4 part 3.75
Sherbet 2.00
Sugar 5.25
Tumbler 4.50

Block Optic

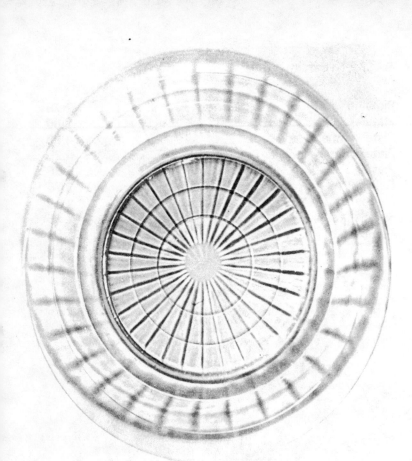

Block Optic

BLOCK OPTIC--------Hocking Glass Co. (1929-1932)

Green, Yellow, Pink, Clear

Bowl - berry	1.00
Bowl - cereal	1.25
Bowl - nappy	2.75
Bowl - serving	3.25
Butter Dish/cover - oblong	4.00
Butter Dish/cover - round	10.50
Candy Dish	5.25
Candle sticks	3.00
Creamer	2.50

BLOCK OPTIC

Cup	2.00
Saucer	1.00
Goblet	2.75
Ice Tub	5.50
Pitcher	7.50
Plate - 6"	1.25
Plate - 8"	1.75
Plate - 9"	2.25
Platter	3.50
Salt & Pepper	5.50
Sherbet	1.75
Sugar - (three styles; cone shaped, footed, & straight)	2.50
Tumbler - 3"	1.00
Tumbler - 4 - 5"	1.50
Tumbler - Iced tea	2.25

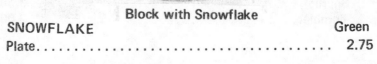

Block with Snowflake

SNOWFLAKE	Green
Plate	2.75

Bowknot

BOWKNOT-------(Unknown Manufacturer)

	Green, Crystal
Bowl	1.50
Cup	2.50
Saucer	1.25
Plate	1.75
Sherbet	1.50
Tumbler	2.00

Bubble

BUBBLE--------(Hocking Glass Co. - 1934-37)

	Pink, Dark Green, Crystal
Bowl - fruit & cereal	1.00
Bowl - soup	1.50
Bowl - serving	2.50
Creamer	2.50
Cup	1.75
Saucer	1.00
Plate - bread & butter	1.00
Plate - dinner	1.75
Platter - 12"	3.00
Sugar	2.50

Bullseye

Bullseye

BULLSEYE

Bowl. 4.50
Tumbler 4.00

Cameo Set

CAMEO--------Hocking Glass (1930-34)

Goblet - 6.00
Pitcher - 6" 10.00
Pitcher - 8" 15.00
Plate - sandwich 4.00
Plate - dinner 3.25
Plate - grill 2.75
Plate - luncheon 2.25
Plate - salad, square 3.75
Plate - sherbet 2.00
Platter 5.50
Relish Dish - 3 part 4.00
Sherbet 2.50
Sherbet - stemmed 4.00
Salt & Pepper. 9.00
Sugar 3.25
Tumbler - juice. 2.50
Tumbler - footed 5.00

Cameo

21

CAMEO

Water Bottle/Stopper (rare) 16.00
Vase (rare) 15.00

Cameo

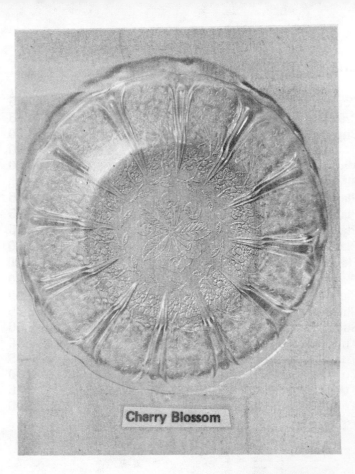

Cherry Blossom

CHERRY BLOSSOM------Jeannette Glass Co. (1930-38)

Pink, Green, Opaque
Blue, Crystal

Bowl - nappy 4" 2.00
Bowl - nappy 5" 2.25
Bowl - nappy 8½" 5.50
Bowl - 3 legged fruit 12.50
Bowl - soup 3.50
Bowl - vegetable/handles 8.00
Bowl - vegetable - oval 5.75
Butter Dish/cover 15.00
Cake stand 9.00

CHERRY BLOSSOM

Coaster	1.75
Creamer	4.75
Cup	4.00
Saucer	2.00
Mug	8.00
Pitcher (3 different kinds)	18.00
Plate - pie	2.75
Plate - salad	2.75
Plate - luncheon	3.25
Plate - dinner	4.00
Plate - grill	5.00
Platter - small	7.00
Platter - large divided	9.00
Sherbet	3.25
Sugar/lid	5.50
Tray	7.50
Tumbler - small	2.25
Tumbler - large	3.00
Tumbler - small footed	3.25
Tumbler - large footed	6.00

Cherry Blossom

Butter Dish/cover (rare)	15.00

24

Cherry Blossom

Junior Set

14 piece set in Pink, Pink Opaque, & Opaque Blue - $175.00
"Delfite"   set

CHECKERBOARD AND WINDMILL

	Green
Ash Tray	2.00
Bowl - nappy	2.50
Bowl - cereal	2.75
Plate	2.50

CHRISTMAS CANDY

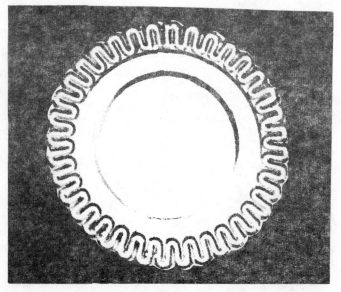

CHRISTMAS CANDY-----Indiana Glass Co. (1936)

Teal blue, Clear, Emerald Green

Creamer	4.50
Plate - pie	3.50
Sugar	4.50

CIRCLE-----Hocking Glass Co.

Pink, Green, Crystal

Creamer	2.00
Cup	1.75
Saucer	1.00
Goblet - wine	2.25
Pitcher	8.00
Plate - dinner	2.25
Plate-- luncheon	2.00
Sherbet	2.25
Sherbet - plate	1.25
Tumbler - 3 sizes	2.25 to 3.50

Cloverleaf

CLOVERLEAF-----Hazel Atlas Co. (1931-35)

Green, Yellow, Pink, Black, Crystal

Ash Tray - set of 4		5.75
Bowl - nappy		2.00
Bowl - vegetable		6.00
Bowl - oval		7.50
Candy Dish/lid		7.00
Creamer	black 7.50	3.00
Cup		3.25
Saucer		1.75
Plate - pie		1.75
Plate - salad		2.00
Plate - luncheon		3.00
Plate - dinner		3.75
Plate - grill		4.00
Salt and Pepper	black 13.00	7.50
Sherbet		2.00
Sugar	black 7.50	3.50
Tumbler - small		4.25
Tumbler - large		5.00

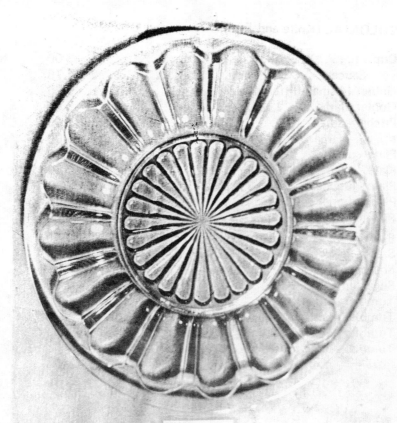

Colonial

COLONIAL (Knife and Fork)
   Hocking Glass Co. (1934-38)

Green, Pink, Crystal

Bowl - nappy - small	2.00
Bowl - nappy - large	6.50
Bowl - soup - small	3.00
Bowl - soup - large	3.50
Bowl - vegetable	7.50
Butter Dish/cover	17.50
Celery or spoon holder	7.50
Creamer	6.00

COLONIAL (Knife and Fork)

Cup 3.00
       Saucer 1.75
Goblet (4 small-different sizes). 5.25
Goblet - large 5.50
Pitcher - small 12.00
Pitcher - large 15.00
Plate - pie. 2.00
Plate - salad 2.75
Plate - luncheon 3.25
Plate - dinner 3.50
Plate - grill 4.00

Platter - 12" 7.50
Salt & Pepper. 9.00
Sherbet 3.50
Sugar/lid 7.50
Tumbler - small 3.00
Tumbler - large. 3.50
Tumbler - small footed 3.25
Tumbler - large footed 5.00

Colonial Fluted

COLONIAL FLUTED ("Rope")
Federal Glass Co. (1928)

	Pink, Green
Bowl - berry	1.50
Bowl - cereal	3.25
Bowl - serving	4.00
Creamer	2.00
Cup	2.00
Saucer	1.25
Plate - pie	1.50
Plate - luncheon	2.00
Platter	5.00
Sherbet	1.75
Sugar/cover	2.50

Columbia

COLUMBIA-------Federal Glass Co. (1938-40)

	Pink, Crystal
Bowl - nappy - small	1.25
Bowl - nappy - large	1.75
Bowl - soup	1.75
Bowl - large	2.50
Butter Dish/cover	12.00
Cup	1.50
Saucer	1.00
Plate - bread & butter	1.25
Plate - luncheon	2.00
Plate - dinner	2.75

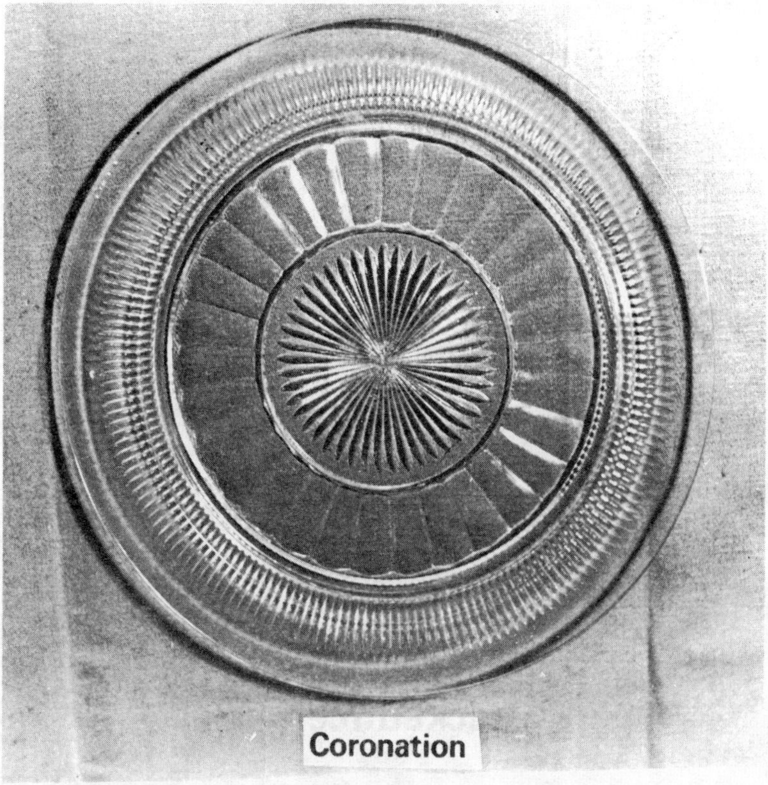

Coronation

CORONATION (Saxon & Banded Fine Ribbed)
    Hocking Glass Co. (1936-1940)

Pink, Crystal, Ruby Red

Bowl - fruit	1.50
Bowl - nappy small	1.50
Bowl - nappy large	4.50
Creamer	2.75
Cup	2.00
Saucer	1.50
Plate - sherbet	1.50
Plate - luncheon	2.00
Platter	5.00
Sherbet - footed	2.00
Sugar	3.00
Tumbler	3.25

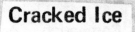

Cracked Ice

CRACKED ICE

	Pink
Creamer & Sugar	5.50

CUBE (Cubist)-----Jeannette Glass Co (1929-1933)

	Pink, Green, Crystal
Bowl - berry	2.00
Bowl - cereal	2.50
Butter dish/cover	15.00
Candy Jar/cover	7.50
Coaster	1.75

CUBE (Cubist)-----Jeannette Glass Co. (1929-1933)

Creamer - small	3.00
Creamer - large	3.00
Cup	2.50
Saucer	1.75
Pitcher	12.00
Plate - sherbet	1.75
Plate - luncheon	2.50
Salt and Pepper	7.50
Sherbet	2.00
Sugar	3.00
Tumbler	3.75

Cubist

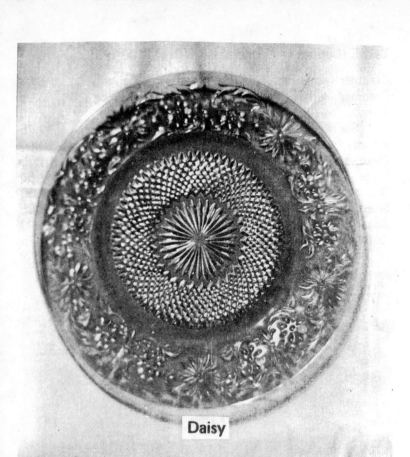

Daisy

DAISY------Indiana Glass Co. (1933-1944)

	Crystal, Amber
Bowl - berry	1.50
Bowl - soup	2.50
Bowl - cereal	1.75
Bowl - vegetable	5.25
Bowl - vegetable - oval	5.75
Creamer	3.25
Cup	2.75
Saucer	2.00
Plate - sherbet	1.50
Plate - salad	2.00

Plate - luncheon 2.25
Plate - dinner 2.75
Plate - grill 3.00
Plate - cake. 5.00
Platter 5.50
Relish Dish - 3 part 4.75
Sherbet 2.00
Sugar 3.25
Tumbler - small 2.75
Tumbler - large. 3.25

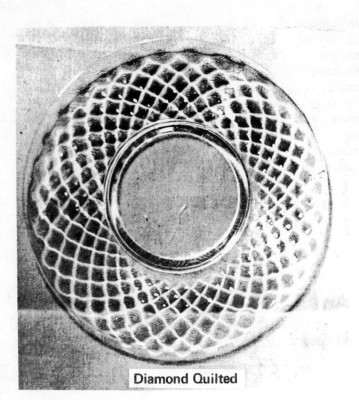

Diamond Quilted

DIAMOND QUILTED------Unknown Manufacturer

Green, Pink, Crystal

Bowl - soup	2.25
Bowl - nappy - small	1.75
Bowl - nappy - large	3.00
Candlesticks	8.50
Creamer	2.75
Cup	2.25
Saucer	1.50
Goblet	4.25
Plate - pie	1.75
Plate - salad	2.00
Plate - luncheon	2.75
Sherbet	2.00
Sugar	3.00
Sherbet in black amethyst (rare)	5.00

Diana

Childs Set - Swirled Sharp Rib, Clear, with Gold Rim
Cup and Saucer Set/frame $150 set
Childs Set - Ruby Red Swirled Sharp Rib
Cup and Saucer $25.00

DIANA (Swirled Sharp Rib)----Federal Glass Co. (1937-1940)

Pink, Amber, Crystal

Ash Tray	2.00
Bowl - nappy - small	1.50
Bowl - nappy - large	4.50
Bowl - soup	1.75
Bowl - vegetable	5.50
Bowl - vegetable - scalloped	7.00
Candy Jar/cover	6.00
Coaster	1.50
Creamer	3.00
Cup	2.75
Saucer	2.00
Demi-Tasse cup & saucer	5.00
Plate - pie	1.75
Plate - dinner	2.75
Plate - cake	3.75
Salt & Pepper	8.00
Sugar	3.25

DOGWOOD------MacBeth-Evans Co. (1928-1932)

Pink, Crystal, Green
Few pieces in Monax

Bowl - cereal	1.75
Bowl - nappy	6.75
Bowl - fruit	7.50
Cake Plate	10.00
Candlesticks	10.00
Creamer	4.50
Cup	3.25
Saucer	2.00
Pitcher - plain	8.00
Pitcher - pattern	17.00
Plate - bread & butter	1.75
Plate - luncheon	2.75
Plate - dinner	3.00
Plate - grill	3.00
Plate - tray	6.75
Platter	8.25
Sherbet - footed	2.00
Sugar	4.50
Tumbler - 4"	3.75
Tumbler - 5"	4.50

Doric

DORIC------- Jeannette Glass Co. (1935-38)

Green, Pink, Crystal,
Opaque Blue

Ash Tray	2.25
Bowl - nappy - small	2.00
Bowl - cereal	2.50
Bowl - nappy - large	5.25
Bowl - oval vegetable	5.50
Bowl - /handles	7.50
Bowl - flared rim	9.00

Butter Dish/cover.............................. 15.00
Cake Plate - 10"............................... 7.50
Candy Dish - 3 part 4.00
Candy Jar/cover............................... 8.50
Coaster 1.75
Creamer 3.25
Condiment Server - Cloverleaf 8.00
Cup 3.25
    Saucer 2.00
Pitcher 9.00
Plate - 9".................................... 3.25
Plate - grill................................. 3.25
Plate - sherbet 2.50
Platter - 12"................................. 6.00
Relish Dishes - 3 sizes.............. 2.50 to 6.50
Salt & Pepper................................. 8.25
Server - handled (fits in tray) 3.00
Sherbet....................................... 4.00
Sugar/cover 3.75
Tray - handles 7.50
Tumbler....................................... 5.00

DORIC AND PANSY-----Jeannette Glass Co. (1937-38)

Pink, Teal-blue, Crystal

Bowl - small nappy 2.50
Bowl - large 7.50
Bowl - oval serving - handled 11.00
Cup 3.25
    Saucer 2.00
Plate - cake 11.00
Plate - 9".................................... 3.75
Plate - 6".................................... 2.50
Sherbet Cup/Saucer............................ 5.00
Tray - handles 10.00
Tumbler 8.00

Doric & Pansy

Junior Dinner Set
Pretty Polly Party Dishes

Green

Creamer	6.00
Cup	4.25
Saucer	2.00
Plate - 6"	2.75
Sugar	6.00
14 piece set	40.00

DOUBLE SHIELD

Cobalt Blue, Black, Amethyst, Clear, Burgundy

Bowl - handled	10.00
Creamer	6.00
Cup	3.50
Saucer	1.75
Plate	3.50
Sugar	7.50
Tray - handle in center	8.00

Double Shield

Double Shield

English Hobnail

ENGLISH HOBNAIL ·······Westmoreland Glass Co. (1925-31)

Pink, Green Amber,
Turquoise, Crystal

Bowl - flared nappy 9.50
Bowl - 8" footed /handles 20.00
Candlesticks 13.50
Candy Dish/cover. 8.25
Compote 9.50
Creamer 7.00
Cup 4.50
Saucer 3.00
Goblet 7.25
Lamp 27.50
Nut Dish/card holder 4.00
Plate - 10" 7.75
Plate - 8" 5.75

ENGLISH HOBNAIL

Plate - 6" 3.25
Relish dish - oblong 6.25
Salt dish - footed 6.50
Salt & Pepper 12.50
Sherbet 4.25
Sugar 7.00
Tumbler - 5" 4.25
Tumbler - 4" 4.00
Tumbler - 3" 3.25

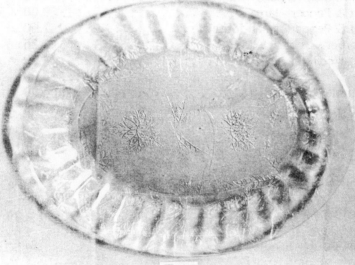

Floral

FLORAL (Poinsettia)----Jeannette Glass Co. (1931-34)

Pink, Green

Ash Tray 2.25
Bowl - 4" berry 2.50
Bowl - 7" nappy 4.25
Bowl - vegetable/lid 7.50
Bowl - vegetable - oval 5.75

47

Butter Dish/cover 17.50
Candlesticks 10.50
Candy Jar/cover 9.50
Coaster 2.00
Creamer 3.75
Cup 3.25
Saucer 2.00
Pitcher - 8" 10.00
Pitcher - 10" 18.50
Plate - dinner 3.25
Plate - salad 2.75
Plate - bread & butter 2.00
Platter 5.75
Relish dish - 2 part/handles 4.75
Salt & Pepper - large 9.00
Salt & Pepper - small-footed 7.50
Sherbet 2.25
Sugar/cover 4.75
Tray 6.00
Tumbler - footed - 3 sizes . . . . 2.25 to 6.00
Vase - 3 legged 13.50

FLORAL & LEAF

Bowl - lily - 3 footed 3.75
Bowl - nut - 3 footed 4.00
Bowl - fruit - handled 4.50
Bowl - serving 3.75
Comport 3.00
Creamer 3.00
Goblet - 9 oz. 3.00
Goblet - 6 oz. 2.50
Goblet - 2 oz. 2.00
Mayonnaise Dish 3.25
Plate - handled - 12" 4.00
Relish - oval, 3 part 3.25
Sherbet 2.25
Tray - handled 4.00
Tumbler - ice tea 3.50

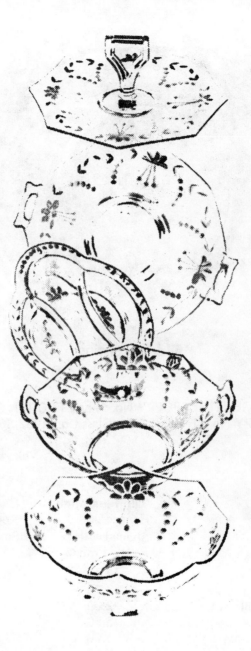

FLORAL & LEAF

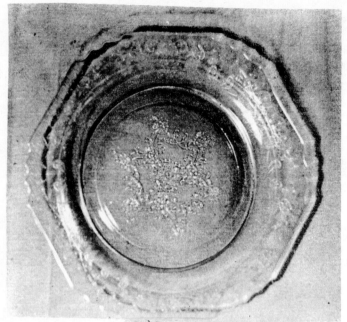

Old Florentine

OLD FLORENTINE (POPPY No. 1) and FLORENTINE (POPPY No. 2) Hazel Atlas Glass Co. (1932-36)

	(Old Florentine) Hexagonal Shaped with Ruffled Edges	Yellow, Green, Pink, Crystal (Florentine) Round & Smooth
Ash Tray	1.75	1.75
Bowl - soup	2.75	2.75
Bowl - small nappy	2.00	2.25
Bowl - large nappy	3.50	5.00
Bowl - oval vegetable	5.00	/cover 7.50
Butter Dish/cover	15.00	16.50
Candlesticks		10.00
Candy Dish/cover		7.50

Comport		4.25
Coasters	2.00	2.25
Creamer	3.00	3.25
Cup	3.00	3.25
Saucer	1.75	2.00
Pitcher	13.25	13.00
Pitcher - large		14.00
Plate - pie	2.00	2.25
Plate - salad	2.50	2.75
Plate - dinner	3.00	3.25
Plate - grill		3.50
Platter	5.25	16.25
Platter/gravy bowl		16.00
Relish dish - 3 part		5.25
Salt & Pepper	8.50	8.50
Sherbet.	2.25	2.50
Sugar /cover	4.25	4.50
Tray-including salt &pepper		
cream & sugar.		16.25

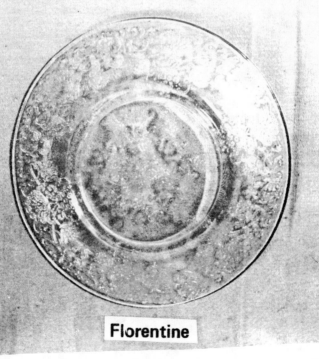

Florentine

Florentine

Tumbler - 3" footed 3.00		3.25
Tumbler - 4"............... 4.75		5.00
Tumbler - 5"............... 5.00		6.00
Vase....................		8.50

FORTUNE------ Hocking Glass Co. (1936-37)

Pink, Crystal

Bowl - nappy	1.25
Bowl - nappy/handle	1.50
Bowl - large nappy	2.50
Candy Dish/cover	4.50
Cup	2.50
Saucer	1.25
Plate - pie	1.75
Plate - luncheon	2.25
Tumbler	2.75

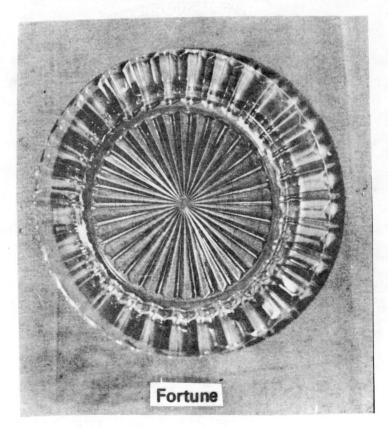

Fortune

FROSTED BLOCK-----Indiana Glass Co. (1920-40)

Yellow, Green, Pink, Clear, Carnival

Bowl - soup, handled	5.50
Creamer	5.00
Cup	3.00
Saucer	1.75
Plate - luncheon	3.50
Sugar	5.50

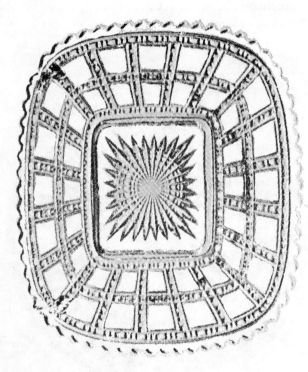

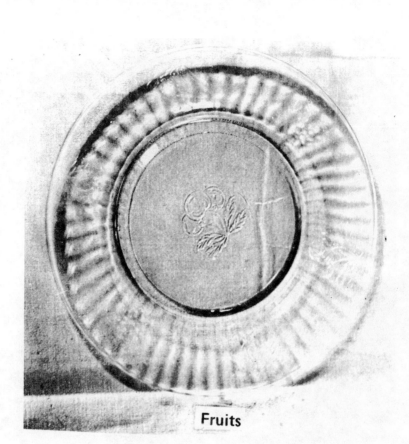

Fruits

FRUITS-----(Unknown Manufacturer)

Pink, Green, Crystal

Bowl - vegetable	7.50
Candleholder	4.00
Cup	3.25
Saucer	2.00
Pitcher	5.00
Plate - Luncheon	3.25
Sherbet	2.75
Tumbler	3.00

3 Fruits

3 Fruits

Salad Plate 3.00

Georgian

GEORGIAN (Love-Birds)------- Federal Glass Co. (1931-35)

	Green
Bowl - 4½"	2.00
Bowl - 6"	2.50
Bowl - 7½"	5.50
Bowl - 9" oval	6.00
Bowl - soup/handles	3.50
Bowl - serving	6.00
Butter Dish/cover	18.50
Creamer - 2 sizes	3.50
Cup	3.00
Saucer	1.75
Hot Plate - 4"	3.75
Plate - 9½"	3.50
Plate - 8"	3.25
Plate - 6"	2.75
Platter	6.50
Sherbet	2.75
Sugar/lid - 2 sizes	5.00
Tumbler - 4" thin	3.25
Tumbler - iced tea	5.00

GOTHIC ARCHES

Amber, Green

Candleholders 8.00
Plate - dessert............................... 2.50

Gothic Arches

Hairpin

HAIRPIN-----Hazel Atlas Glass Co.

Cobalt Blue, Milk Glass, Amethyst

Creamer	4.00
Cup	3.00
Saucer	1.75
Plate	3.50
Plate - dessert	2.75
Sherbet	2.75
Sugar	4.50

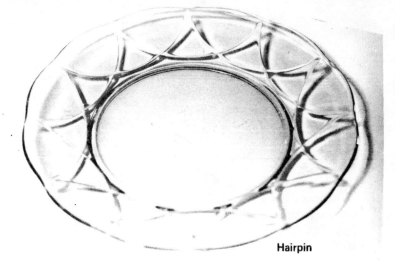

Hairpin

Heritage

HERITAGE -------- Federal Glass Co. (1940)

Crystal

Bowl - fruit	5.00
Bowl - 8½"	3.50
Bowl - 5"	2.00
Cup	2.50
Saucer	1.25
Plate - sherbet	1.50
Plate - luncheon	3.00
Plate 12" sandwich	3.50

Hobnail

HOBNAIL------- Hocking Glass Co. (1934-1936)

Crystal (few pieces
in pink)

Bowl - 7″	2.75
Bowl - 5½″ cereal	1.50
Creamer	2.75
Cup	2.50
Saucer	1.25
Decanter/stopper	9.50
Goblet	3.00

Goblet - iced tea............................... 3.75
Pitcher 5.00
Pitcher - jug 7.50
Plate - luncheon 2.50
Plate - sherbet 1.50
Sherbet 2.00
Sugar 2.75
Tumbler - small 2.00
Tumbler - large.............................. 2.25
Tumbler - footed, small 2.25
Tumbler - footed, large...................... 2.50

HOLIDAY (Buttons & Bows)----Jeannette Glass Co. (1947-1949)

	Pink
Bowl - console	12.00
Bowl - berry	2.00
Bowl - fruit	5.50
Bowl - cereal	2.75
Bowl - vegetable, oval	5.50
Butter Dish/cover	20.00
Cake Plate - 10½"	7.50

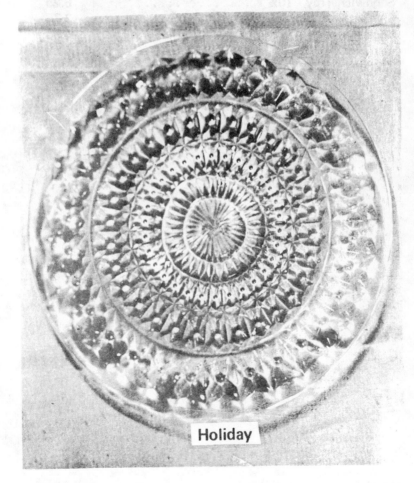

Holiday

Candlesticks 10.00
Creamer 3.25
Cup 3.00
      Saucer 1.75
Goblet 6.00
Pitcher 4½" 6.50
Pitcher 7" 12.50
Plate - chop 10.50
Plate - dinner 3.50
Plate - sherbet 2.25
Platter 5.50
Sandwich Tray - 10½" 6.25
Sherbet 2.75
Sugar/cover 4.50
Tumbler - 4" 4.50
Tumbler - 6" 5.00

HOMESPUN------ Jeannette Glass Co. (1938-1940)

Pink

Bowl - nappy	2.00
Bowl - cereal	2.25
Bowl - serving	6.00
Butter Dish/cover	13.00
Coaster	1.50
Creamer	3.25
Cup	3.00
Saucer	1.75

Homespun

```
Pitcher ................................. 10.00
Plate - dinner ............................ 3.25
Plate - salad ............................. 2.75
Plate - sherbet ........................... 2.00
Platter 13" ............................... 6.25
Sherbet .................................. 2.00
Sugar .................................... 3.75
Tumbler - 4" .............................. 3.25
Tumbler - 5½" ............................ 4.00
Tumbler - 4" footed ....................... 4.25
Tumbler - 6" footed ....................... 4.50
```

```
Tea Set (Pink & Crystal) ................... 30.00
        Consists of:
        4 cups & saucers
        4 plates
        1 teapot/cover
```

Homespun

Mustard Jar/chrome top 10.00

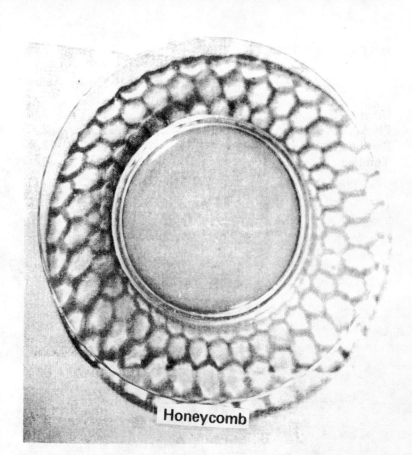

Honeycomb

HONEYCOMB------- Federal Glass Co. (1929-1932)

Green, Pink

Bowl - nappy	5.00
Creamer	3.00
Cup	2.25
Saucer	1.50
Pitcher	13.50
Plate - luncheon	2.25
Plate - pie	1.50
Salt Shaker	4.50
Sugar	3.00
Tumbler	5.00

IMITATION CRACKLE

Pink, Green, Clear, Dark Green, Amber

Bowl 3.50
Plate.................................... 2.75
Sherbet.................................. 2.50
Tumbler................................. 4.00

Imitation Crackle

INTAGLIO

	Clear
Creamer	2.75
Cup	2.25
Saucer	1.00
Plate - salad	2.50
Plate - cake	4.00
Sugar	3.00

IRIS AND HERRINGBONE-----Jeannette Glass Co. (1928-1950)

Green, Pink, Clear, Iridescent Marigold

Bowl - dessert	3.00
Bowl - fluted	3.50
Butter Dish/cover	8.00
Candlesticks	5.00
Candy Dish/cover/handles	9.00
Creamer	3.00

Iris & Herringbone

Cup	2.50
Saucer	1.25
Pitcher	9.00
Plate - sandwich	3.25
Plate - dinner	3.00
Plate - luncheon	2.50
Plate - dessert	2.00
Platter	5.00
Sherbet	2.75
Sugar/cover	3.25
Tumbler - 4"	2.25
Tumbler - 4" footed	2.50
Tumbler - ice tea - footed	3.25
Vase	6.50

Lace Edge

LACE EDGE (Open Lace)-----Hocking Glass Co. (1935-1938)

Pink, Crystal

Bowl - 3 leg	9.00
Bowl - 9½" nappy	6.50
Bowl - 7½" nappy	4.00
Bowl - cereal	3.00
Butter Dish/cover.	20.00
Candlesticks.	8.00
Candy jar/cover	8.00
Comport/cover.	7.00
Cookie jar/cover.	9.00
Creamer	3.25
Cup	3.25
Saucer	1.75
Flower Bowl/frog.	5.50
Plate - dinner	3.25
Plate - grill	3.25

71

Plate - salad 2.75
Plate - bread & butter....................... 2.25
Plate - relish - 3 parts 3.75
Plate - 13" relish - 5 parts................. 7.25
Platter 6.00
Preserve dish/cover......................... 12.50
Relish plate 5.25
Sandwich Server............................ 15.00
Sherbet 2.75
Sugar 3.50
Tumbler................................... 4.25
Vase - 7" 8.00

Lace Edge

Leaf

LEAF-----MacBeth-Evans Glass Co.

Green, Pink, Clear

Plate....................................... 3.50

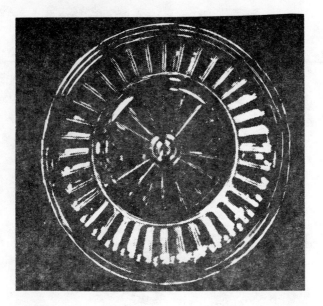

LYDIA RAY------Unknown Manufacturer

Crystal, Green, Burgundy,
Dark Blue

Bowl - 5" 1.25
Bowl - 8" 5.00
Butter Dish/cover. 13.50
Creamer 3.25
Cup 1.75
      Saucer 1.00
Plate - luncheon 2.25
Plate - sherbet 1.50
Salt & Pepper. 7.00
Sugar 3.50
Tumbler - 5". 2.75
Tumbler - 4". 2.25
Tumbler - 3". 1.75

Madrid

MADRID------- Federal Glass Co. (1932-38)

	Amber, Pink Green, Crystal	Blue
Bowl - soup/handles	2.25	4.25
Bowl - cereal	2.25	4.25
Bowl - nappy - 5"	2.00	3.50
Bowl - nappy - 8"	5.25	9.00
Bowl - fruit - 9"	6.50	9.25
Bowl - 10" deep salad	10.25	
Bowl - vegetable - oval	6.50	9.00
Bowl - 11" flared console	8.25	10.00
Butter Dish/cover	17.25	18.00
Cake Plate	7.50	10.00
Candlesticks	10.00	13.00
Coaster - 5"	5.25	6.75
Cracker Jar/cover	12.50	15.00
Creamer	3.50	6.00
Cup	3.25	5.00
Saucer	2.00	2.50
Jelly Dish - 7"	4.25	6.00

Jello Mold	4.00	6.00
Pitcher - 5"	8.25	11.00
Pitcher - 8" square	12.50	15.00
Pitcher - 8½" jug	15.00	16.50
Pitcher - 8½" ice jug	15.00	16.50
Plate - grill	3.25	5.50
Plate - relish	3.50	
Plate - dinner	3.25	5.25
Plate - luncheon	2.50	4.00
Plate - salad	2.50	3.50
Plate - bread & butter	2.25	2.75
Platter - 11½"	4.25	7.50

Madrid

Salt and Pepper (2 styles-flat & footed 8.00		10.25
Sherbet 2.25		4.00
Sherbet Plate - off-center for cup 1.50		1.50
Sugar/cover 4.75		6.75
Tumbler - 4"............... 2.25		3.00
Tumbler - 4" footed......... 2.50		3.00
Tumbler - 4½" footed 2.75		3.25
Tumbler - 5½" 3.25		4.75
Tumbler - 5½" footed 4.00		5.50

Madrid

MANHATTAN ("Ribbed Horizontal")-----Anchor Hocking Co. (1939-1941)

	Pink	Crystal
Ash Tray	1.75	1.00
Bowl - 4½"................	1.75	1.50
Bowl - 5½"................	2.00	1.50
Bowl - 9"	5.25	3.75
Bowl - 9½"/handles	6.00	4.00
Candlesticks...............	7.50	4.25
Coaster...................	1.75	.75
Compote	4.25	2.75
Creamer..................	3.25	2.00

Cup	2.25	1.50
Saucer	1.75	1.25
Lazy Susan-divided 5 parts	8.00	5.75
Pitcher - fruit juice	6.00	3.50
Pitcher - ice jug	7.50	4.25
Plate - salad	2.50	1.75
Plate - sherbet	2.00	1.25
Plate - dinner	3.50	2.50
Plate - sandwich	6.00	3.75
Plate - relish-4 parts	6.25	4.00
Salt & Pepper	6.50	3.75
Sherbet	2.00	1.50
Sugar	3.50	2.75
Tumbler - footed	3.25	2.50
Vase	7.25	4.00

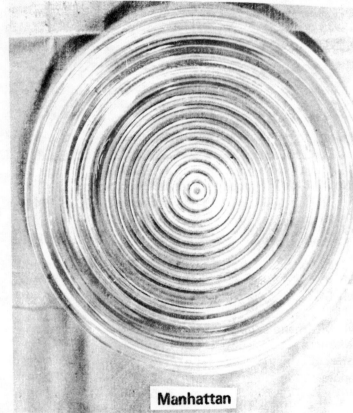

Manhattan

MAYFAIR------Federal Glass Co. (1934)

Amber, Crystal

Bowl - nappy	2.50
Bowl - cereal	2.75
Bowl - oval vegetable	6.50
Creamer	3.25
Cup	3.25
Saucer	2.00
Plate - dinner	3.25
Plate - salad	2.00
Platter	7.25
Sugar	3.25
Tumbler	5.25

Mayfair (Federal)

MAYFAIR (Open Rose)-----Hocking Glass Co. (1931-1936)

	Pink	Blue
Bowl - soup	3.00	
Bowl - fruit	2.75	3.75
Bowl - nappy	3.75	6.75
Bowl - oval vegetable	5.50	7.75
Bowl - handles	5.75	10.00
Bowl - vegetable/lid	11.50	15.00
Bowl - flat	9.00	14.25
Bowl - 12"-flared	9.00	14.00
Butter Dish/cover	18.50	20.00
Cake Plate - footed	8.00	11.50
Candy Jar/Lid-footed	10.00	13.50
Celery Plate - 2 part	7.00	11.00
Cracker Jar/cover	9.00	15.00

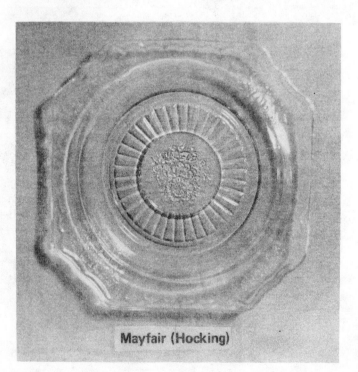

Mayfair (Hocking)

Creamer	4.50	9.00
Cup	3.25	5.00
Saucer	2.25	3.50
Goblet - 6" stemmed		8.50

Mayfair (Hocking)

Pitcher - 6" juice	8.00	12.50
Pitcher - 8"	12.00	16.00
Pitcher - 8½"	15.00	19.00
Plate - bread & butter	2.00	3.00
Plate - sherbet	2.00	3.00
Plate - luncheon	3.00	4.25
Plate - grill	3.75	5.50
Plate - dinner	4.00	7.00
Plate - cake/handles	9.00	12.50
Platter - 12"	5.00	8.50
Relish - 4 part	6.00	9.00
Salt & Pepper	7.50	13.50

Sandwich Plate-handle in center	9.00	11.75
Sherbet	3.00	4.25
Sherbet - long stemmed	4.00	6.00
Sugar	4.00	8.25
Tumbler - 2¼" jigger	2.75	
Tumbler - 3½"	2.75	4.50
Tumbler - 4"	3.25	6.00
Tumbler - 4" cocktail........	4.25	
Tumbler - 5¼"..............	4.25	7.00
Tumbler - 4½" wine	4.25	
Tumbler - 5¾"..............	5.25	
Tumbler - 7¼"...............	6.00	8.25
Tumbler - 3¼" footed	3.25	
Tumbler - 5½" footed	4.00	7.25
Tumbler - 6½" footed	5.00	8.25
Vase - hat shaped	15.00	30.00
Wine Decanter/stopper.......	25.00	

MAYFLOWER

Serving Plate 3.00

MISS AMERICA-------Hocking Glass Co. (1933-1936)

	Pink	Clear	Green
Bowl - 10" oval vegetable...	7.50	7.50	
Bowl - deep dish..........	15.00	15.00	20.00
Bowl - 8" curved top	21.00	21.00	
Bowl - nappy			3.25
Bowl - cereal	3.50	3.00	4.75
Butter Dish/cover.........	24.00	24.00	
Cake Plate - footed........	13.00	13.00	
Candy Jar/cover..........	25.00	23.00	

Miss America

Candlesticks	12.00	12.00
Celery Dish - oblong.......	7.50	5.25
Coaster................	2.50	2.00
Compote	24.00	20.00
Compote on Pedestal	5.00	4.50
Creamer	6.00	5.75

Cup	5.25	4.50	5.00
Saucer	2.50	2.25	2.25
Goblet - water	7.50	6.75	
Goblet - wine	5.25		
Goblet - juice	4.50	4.50	
Pitcher - 8½" with ice lip	30.00	30.00	
Pitcher - 8½" without ice lip	30.00	30.00	
Plate - 5¾"	2.75	2.00	2.50
Plate - 8½" salad	4.00	3.75	4.00
Plate - grill	5.50	5.00	
Plate - dinner	6.00	5.50	
Platter - 12"	7.50	7.50	
Relish - 4 part round	5.50	5.50	
Relish - divided round		6.00	
Salt and Pepper	11.00	9.75	
6 Salt dips with tray - center handle		47.50 set	
Sherbet	4.50	4.00	4.50
Sugar	7.50	7.50	
Tumbler - juice	4.00	3.50	
Tumbler - 4"	4.50	4.00	4.00
Tumbler - 6"	6.25	5.50	

MODERNTONE------Hazel Atlas Glass Co. (1934-37)

Cobalt Blue, Burgundy

Bowl - 8" nappy	5.00
Bowl - 6"	3.00
Bowl - 4"	2.50
Butter Dish/Chrome Top	15.00
Creamer	3.25
Cup	3.50
Saucer	1.75
Plate - dinner	3.00
Plate - salad	2.50
Plate - sherbet	2.00
Plate - cake	5.00
Platter	5.50
Salt and Pepper	8.00
Sherbet	3.25
Sugar	3.75

Moderntone

MOONSTONE-----Anchor-Hocking Glass Co. (1936-40)

Pink, Blue-white, Opalescent Hobnail

Bonbon	3.75
Bowl - fluted	3.50
Bowl - dessert	4.00
Bowl - handled	4.00
Candlesticks	4.25
Candy Jar/cover	10.00
Creamer	3.25
Cup	3.00
Saucer	1.75
Goblet	3.25
Plate - 10" Sandwich	4.00
Plate - luncheon	3.00
Plate - dessert	2.50
Puff Box/cover	6.50
Relish Dish - divided	3.75
Salt and Pepper	6.00
Sherbet	3.00
Sherbet - plate	1.75
Sugar	3.50
Vase	7.00

New Century

NEW CENTURY------Hazel Atlas Glass Co. (1930)

Green

Bowl - small nappy	1.25
Bowl - large nappy	1.75
Bowl - fruit, footed	2.00
Creamer	2.25
Cup	2.00
Saucer	1.25
Plate - luncheon	2.25
Sherbet	2.00
Sugar	2.25

NORMANDIE (Bouquet and Lattice)
Federal Glass Co. (1933-39)

	Pink, Amber, Green, Clear	Sunburst (Carnival)
Bowl - cereal	5.50	7.50
Bowl - 5" berry	2.50	3.00
Bowl - serving	5.00	6.00
Bowl - oval vegetable	6.00	8.00
Creamer	3.25	6.00
Cup	3.00	4.00
Saucer	2.00	2.50
Pitcher - 8" jug (rare)	15.00	
Plate - dinner	3.75	5.00
Plate - grill	3.75	5.00
Plate - luncheon	3.00	4.00
Plate - salad	2.50	3.25
Plate - bread and butter	2.25	3.00
Platter - 12"	6.00	7.00
Salt and Pepper	8.00	
Sherbet - footed	2.25	3.50
Sugar	3.50	6.25
Tumbler - 5"	5.50	
Tumbler - 4½"	5.00	
Tumbler - 4"	4.75	

Normandie

Normandie

NUMBER 612 (Horseshoe)--Indiana Glass Co. (1930-33)

Green, Yellow

Bowl - oval vegetable 5.75
Bowl - 9" 6.00
Bowl - 7½" nappy 5.25
Bowl - cereal 2.75
Bowl - berry 2.50
Creamer 4.25

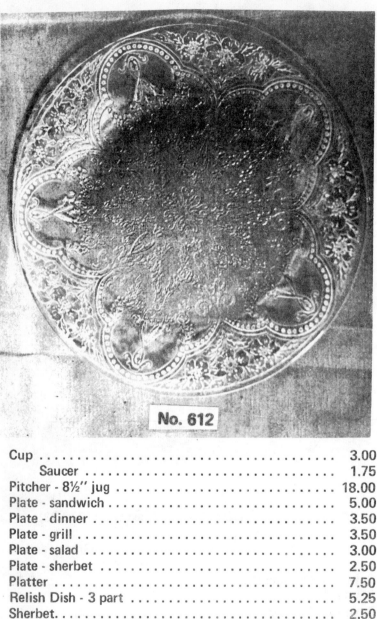

No. 612

Cup	3.00
Saucer	1.75
Pitcher - 8½″ jug	18.00
Plate - sandwich	5.00
Plate - dinner	3.50
Plate - grill	3.50
Plate - salad	3.00
Plate - sherbet	2.50
Platter	7.50
Relish Dish - 3 part	5.25
Sherbet.	2.50
Sugar	4.50
Tumbler - 12 oz. footed	3.75
Tumbler - 9 oz. footed	3.25

OLD CAFE-----Hocking Glass Co. (1936-38)

	Pink, Clear	Ruby Red
Bowl - 9"	4.00	
Bowl - 8" oval vegetable......		5.25
Bowl - 8" nappy............		4.75
Bowl - soup................		3.00
Bowl - 5" cereal	2.25	
Bowl - 4" berry.............	2.00	4.00
Candy Dish - flared..........	3.50	5.00
Creamer - 2 styles...........		3.50
Cup	2.50	5.00
Saucer	1.50	3.00
Olive Dish - oblong	2.50	
Pitcher - round tilted		6.00
Pitcher - 3 qt...............		8.00

Plate - dinner	3.25	6.00
Plate - salad		3.50
Plate - sherbet.	1.25	3.00
Salt and Pepper	7.50	
Sherbet.	2.25	4.50
Sugar - 2 styles		3.75
Tumbler - cocktail		2.75
Tumbler - juice.	2.25	4.00
Tumbler - 4".	2.50	
Tumbler - 10"		4.00
Tumbler - footed wine		3.75
Vase.		8.00

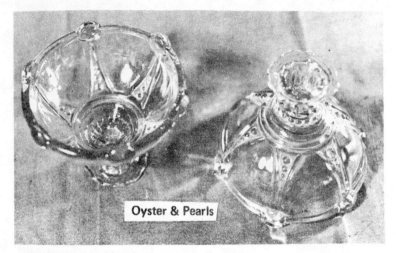

Oyster & Pearls

OYSTER AND PEARLS----Hocking Glass Co. (1938-40)

	Pink, Clear, white with pink or green	Ruby Red
Bowl - fruit	7.50	14.00
Bowl - deep/handled.	4.50	9.00
Bowl - spout/one handle	3.25	
Bowl - round	2.50	5.00
Candlesticks.	6.50	12.00
Candy Dish	3.00	
Plate - sandwich	6.00	11.00
Relish - oval divided	5.50	

Parrot

PARROT------Federal Glass Co. (1932)

Green, Yellow

Bowl - oval vegetable	7.00
Bowl - 8½" nappy	6.25
Bowl - 5" nappy	3.00
Bowl - soup	3.75
Butter Dish/cover	16.50
Creamer	5.50
Cup	3.25
Saucer	2.00
Jelly Dish	3.50
Plate - grill	5.25
Plate - dinner	5.00
Plate - salad	3.75
Plate - sherbet	2.75
Platter - 11"	8.00
Salt and Pepper	9.00
Sherbet	3.00
Sugar/cover	5.50
Tumbler	6.25

93

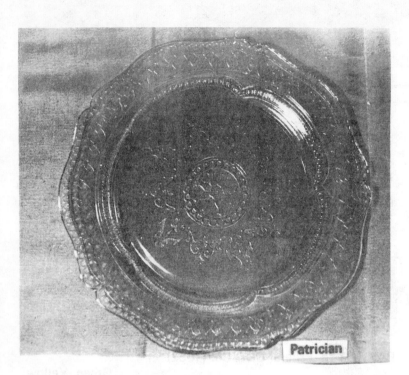

Patrician

PATRICIAN (Spoke)-----Federal Glass Co. (1933-37)

	Green, Pink, Amber, Clear
Bowl - 10" oval	6.00
Bowl - 8½" nappy	5.75
Bowl - soup	4.75
Bowl - cereal	4.50
Bowl - berry	4.25
Butter dish/cover	19.00
Cookie Jar/cover	13.50
Creamer	3.25
Cup	3.75
Saucer	2.00
Jelly Dish	3.75

Pitcher	15.00
Plate - dinner	4.00
Plate - grill	3.75
Plate - luncheon	3.00
Plate - salad	2.75
Plate - bread and butter	2.25
Platter	6.00
Salt and Pepper	9.00
Sherbet	2.50
Sugar/cover	5.00
Tumbler - 5 oz.	2.75
Tumbler - 9 oz.	3.25
Tumbler - 12 oz.	4.00
Tumbler - footed	4.25

PETALWARE (Petal) - Macbeth-Evans (1930-36)

	Pink, Clear	Monax
Bowl - oval vegetable	5.50	8.25
Bowl - 8"	5.25	8.00
Bowl - cereal	3.00	4.00
Bowl - soup	3.25	4.00

Petalware

	Pink, Crystal	Monax
Butter Dish/cover	19.00	25.00
Creamer	3.25	4.50
Cup	3.25	4.50
Saucer	1.75	2.25
Plate - 12"		7.50
Plate - 11" sandwich	4.50	6.00
Plate - dinner	3.25	5.00
Plate - salad	2.75	3.50
Plate - bread and butter	2.50	3.00
Platter - 13"	6.00	8.50
Salt and Pepper	6.50	10.00
Sherbet - footed	2.50	3.00
Sugar	3.50	4.75

PINEAPPLE AND FLORAL-----Indiana Glass Co. (1932-37)

	Clear	Amber
Ash Tray	1.00	1.50
Bowl - oval vegetable	3.75	5.50
Bowl - berry - deep	3.50	5.25
Bowl - cereal	2.50	3.00
Compote	2.00	3.00
Creamer	3.25	3.50
Cup	2.50	3.00
Saucer	1.50	2.25
Plate - 2 tier with handle in center	8.50	12.00
Plate - cake	4.50	5.00
Plate - dinner	2.75	3.25
Plate - salad	2.50	3.00
Plate - sherbet	2.00	2.50
Platter	3.50	4.75
Relish Dish	2.75	3.50
Sherbet	2.50	2.75
Sugar	3.50	3.75
Tumbler	2.50	3.00
Tumbler - iced tea	3.00	3.50

PRINCESS-----Hocking Glass Co. (1931-34)

Green, Pink, Yellow, pieces in satin finish

Ash Tray	2.00
Bowl - oval vegetable	5.25
Bowl - hat-shaped	8.00
Bowl - salad, octagon shaped	6.75
Bowl - cereal	3.00
Bowl - soup	2.75
Butter Dish/cover	19.00
Cake Plate - footed	8.50
Candy Jar/cover	12.00
Cookie Jar/cover	12.00
Creamer	3.25
Cup (green/platinum border - rare)	3.25
Saucer	2.00
Pitcher - 5"	12.00
Pitcher - 8"	18.00
Plate - sandwich, handles	4.00
Plate - grill, handles	5.50
Plate - grill	5.00
Plate - dinner	3.50
Plate - salad	3.00
Plate - sherbet	2.50
Platter	6.50
Relish Dish - 4 part	6.00

Princess

Salt and Pepper	9.00
Sherbet	3.50
Spice Shaker - (green)	6.00
Sugar/cover	4.50
Tumbler - iced tea	5.00
Tumbler - footed	4.00
Tumbler - 5"	3.50
Tumbler - 4"	3.00
Tumbler - 3"	2.50
Vase	10.00

Princess/Platinum Rim
(Rare)

QUEEN ANNE-----Hocking Glass Co.

Ice Tea pitcher. 10.00
Ice Tea Tumbler. 2.50

Queen Anne

QUEEN MARY (Vertical Rib)---Hocking Glass Co. (1936-39)

Pink, Clear

Ash Tray	1.50
Bowl - 9"	4.50
Bowl - 6" with rim...........................	2.00
Bowl - 7" nappy.............................	3.25
Bowl - 4" nappy.............................	2.00
Bowl - 6" 2-handles	2.25

Queen Mary

Bowl - 4" 1-handle...........................	1.75
Candlesticks - 2 candle......................	4.50
Candy Jar/cover.............................	7.50
Cigarette Dish - oval........................	2.25
Coaster.....................................	1.50
Compote	5.25
Creamer	3.25

Cup	2.75
Saucer	1.25
Pickle Dish	4.25
Plate - sandwich	5.50
Plate - dinner	3.25
Plate - salad	2.50
Plate - sherbet	1.75
Platter	5.00
Preserve Dish/cover	8.00
Relish Dish - 4 part	5.00
Relish Dish - 3 part	5.00
Salt and Pepper	5.50
Sherbet	1.50
Sugar	3.50
Tumbler - juice	2.75
Tumbler - 4"	4.00
Tumbler - footed	5.00

RADIANCE

Crystal, Ruby Red

Creamer	4.00
Cup	3.00
Saucer	2.00
Plate - salad	3.25
Plate - sandwich	4.75
Sugar	4.50

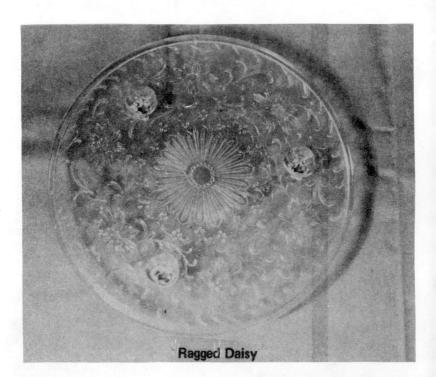
Ragged Daisy

RAGGED DAISY

Green, Pink

Cake Stand. 4.50

RAINDROPS----Federal Glass Co. (1929-32)

	Green
Bowl	1.75
Creamer	2.50
Cup	1.75
Saucer	1.00
Plate - dinner	2.25
Plate - dessert	1.50
Sugar	2.25

Raindrops

RIBBON-----Hazel Atlas Glass Co. (1930-31)

Green, Milk Glass

Bowl - 8½" deep bowl	6.00
Candy Dish/cover	8.00
Creamer	3.25
Cup	3.25
Saucer	2.00
Plate - 8"	3.50
Plate - 6"	2.50
Salt and Pepper	6.00
Sherbet	2.75
Sugar	3.50
Tumbler - footed	3.25

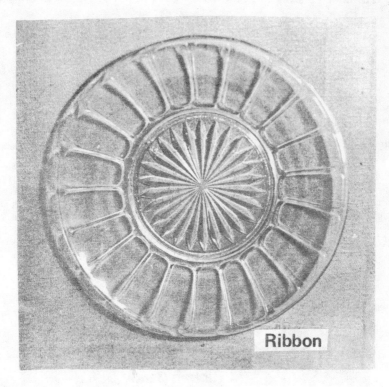

Ribbon

RIBBON CANDY----Indiana Glass Co. (1935)

Clear

Bowl - 7" soup - one handle	3.50
Bowl - berry	4.00
Creamer	3.00
Cup	2.00
Saucer	1.25
Olive Dish - handle	2.00
Pickle Dish - handle	2.00
Plate - dinner	2.50
Plate - cake	4.00
Plate - luncheon - one handle	3.50
Plate - salad	3.00
Plate - dessert	2.50
Sugar	3.25
Tumbler - 3 sizes	3.00 to 6.00

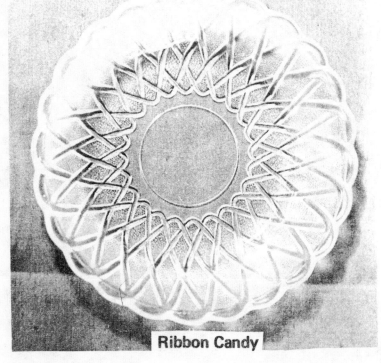

Ribbon Candy

RING-----Hocking Glass Co. (1927-32)

Green, Clear,
Clear with platinum rim,
Clear with black, red, yellow rings

Bowl - 8" 4.50
Bowl - 5" 1.50
Cocktail mixer 9.25

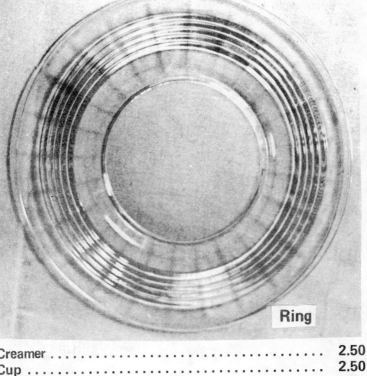

Ring

Creamer 2.50
Cup 2.50
　　Saucer 1.25
Decanter with stopper 10.00
Goblet - stemmed.............................. 4.50
Ice Bucket 6.00
Pitcher - 8" 9.00
Pitcher - 9" 10.50
Plate - luncheon 2.75

```
Plate - sherbet .................................  2.00
Plate - 6" ...................................  1.50
Salt and Pepper...............................  5.00
Sandwich tray with center handle ..............  6.50
Sherbet ......................................  2.00
Sherbet - stemmed ...........................  2.50
Sugar ........................................  3.00
Tumbler - 3 sizes .........................  2.00-3.50
Tumbler - footed - 3 sizes..................  3.25-4.75
```

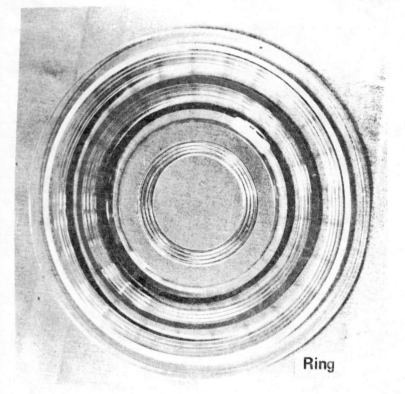

Ring

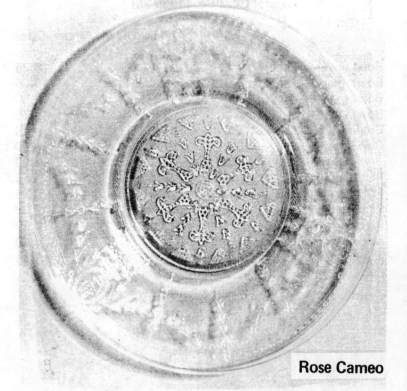

Rose Cameo

ROSE CAMEO------Unknown origin

	Green
Bowl - 4"	2.00
Bowl - 5"	2.75
Cup	3.25
Saucer	1.75
Ice Bowl	5.00
Plate - luncheon	3.25
Plate - salad	2.75
Plate - pie	2.00
Sherbet	2.25
Tumbler - cone-shaped/footed	3.50

ROSEMARY (Dutch Rose)
Federal Glass Co. (1935-36)

Pink, Green, Amber, Clear

Bowl - oval vegetable 6.25
Bowl - nappy 3.00
Bowl - soup 2.50
Bowl - cereal. 2.75
Creamer 3.75
Cup 3.00
      Saucer 2.00
Plate - dinner 3.75
Plate - grill 3.25
Plate - salad 2.00
Platter 6.50
Sugar 4.00
Tumbler 5.25

Rosemary

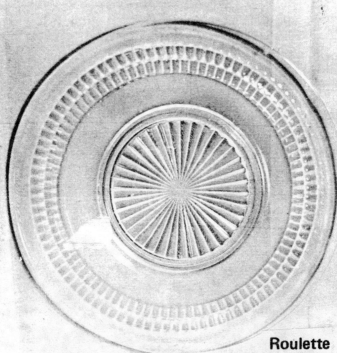

Roulette

ROULETTE-----Hocking Glass Co. (1936-38)

Green, Pink

Bowl - fruit 5.00
Cup 2.25
      Saucer 1.50
Pitcher 12.00
Plate - 12".................................... 3.50
Plate - 8½".................................... 2.50
Plate - 6" 1.75
Sherbet 2.25
Tumbler - 5 sizes 2.00-3.50
Tumbler - footed 3.50

ROUND ROBIN-----Manufacturer Unknown

	Green
Bowl - 4"	1.50
Creamer	3.00
Cup	2.25
Saucer	1.25
Plate - 8"	2.75
Plate - 6"	1.50
Sugar	3.25

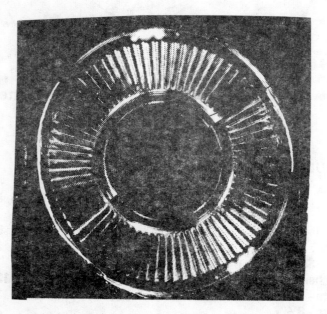

ROXANA-----Manufacturer Unknown

	Yellow
Plate	2.25
Sherbet	2.00
Tumbler	2.75

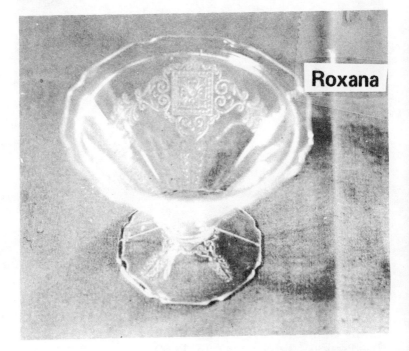

ROYAL LACE-----Hazel Atlas Glass Co. (1934-41)

	Pink, Green, Clear	Cobalt Blue
Ash Tray	2.00	2.75
Bowl - oval vegetable	6.00	15.00
Bowl - nappy - 10"	4.75	12.00
Bowl - nappy - 6"	2.75	6.00
Bowl - nappy - 5" handled	2.75	5.25
Bowl - soup - 5"	2.75	6.00
Bowl - 10" rolled rim	12.00	16.00
Bowl - 3-legged - 10"	10.00	20.00

Royal Lace

Bowl - 3-legged - ruffled	12.00	24.00
Butter Dish/cover	18.00	25.00
Candlesticks - 3 styles	11.00	15.00
Cookie Jar/cover	10.00	20.00
Creamer	5.25	7.50
Cup	3.25	6.50
Saucer	1.50	3.00
Pitcher - 2 styles	15.00	30.00
Plate - 10"	4.50	8.00
Plate - grill	4.50	8.00
Plate - 8"	3.25	6.00
Plate - 7"	2.50	5.00
Plate - 6"	2.25	4.00
Platter	8.50	14.00
Salt and Pepper	11.00	16.00

Sherbet	2.50	5.00
Sugar/cover	5.50	10.00
Tumbler - 3"	4.00	7.00
Tumbler - 4"	5.00	9.00
Tumbler - 5"	6.00	11.00
Cookie Jar/lid in Amethyst		20.00
Sundae Dish-chrome/clear liner (rare)		12.50

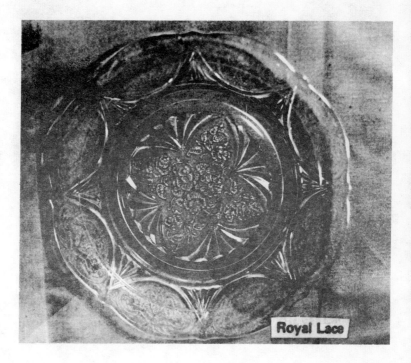

Royal Lace

Royal Lace

S-PATTERN-----MacBeth-Evans Glass Co. (1930-32)

Pink, Yellow, Clear, &
Clear with blue trim or gold trim or platinum trim

Bowl - 8½"......................................	5.50
Bowl - 5½"......................................	2.75
Cake Plate	7.50
Creamer - 2 styles..............................	3.75
Cup	3.00
Saucer	1.75
Pitcher	13.50
Plate - grill	3.25
Plate - 8"	2.50
Plate - 6"	2.00
Sherbet - footed...............................	2.25
Sugar - 2 styles................................	4.00
Tumbler - juice................................	2.25
Tumbler - ice tea	3.25

S-Pattern

Sandwich
Hocking

SANDWICH------Anchor Hocking Glass Co. (1940)

	Clear	Amber, Dark Green
Bowl - fruit	3.00	4.00
Bowl - oval vegetable	3.50	4.00
Bowl - serving	3.00	3.50
Bowl - salad	2.25	3.25
Bowl - nappy	2.25	2.25
Bowl - soup	2.00	2.25
Bowl - berry	1.25	1.75
Butter Dish/cover.	15.75	
Cookie Jar/cover	8.50	12.00
Creamer	2.50	3.75
Cup	2.25	2.50
Saucer	1.00	1.75
Pitcher.	12.00	15.00
Plate - 12".	3.50	5.00

Plate - 9" 2.50	3.75
Plate - 9"/cup............. 3.50	
Plate - 7" 2.00	2.50
Sherbet 1.25	2.00
Sugar/cover 3.50	4.75
Tumbler - juice............ 1.50	1.75
Tumbler - ice tea 1.75	2.00
Tumbler - footed 2.75	
Punch Bowl & 6 cups........ 12.50	

Sandwich
Hocking

SANDWICH-----Indiana Glass Co. (1930)

Pink, Amber, Green, Clear

Ash Tray (set of 4)	4.75
Bowl - console ruffled	7.50
Bowl - console	7.50
Bowl - serving	5.25
Bowl - serving - hexagon shaped	2.50
Bowl - deep	2.75
Bowl - soup	2.75
Bowl/ladle	7.50
Butter Dish/cover	22.00
Candlesticks - short	7.50
Candlesticks - tall	9.75
Creamer	3.50
Cruet	4.50
Cup	3.00
Saucer	1.75
Goblet - wine	2.25

Sandwich
Indiana

Goblet - water.	4.75
Pitcher	12.00
Plate - cake	7.50
Plate - dinner	5.00
Plate - oval	6.00
Plate - salad	3.25
Plate - bread & butter.	3.00
Plate - dessert	2.00
Puff Box/cover.	6.50
Sherbet	2.25
Sugar/cover	4.75
Sugar/creamer/Tray	7.50
Tray - celery.	3.50
Tray - serving	6.00
Tray - sandwich/center handle	10.00
Tumbler - wine.	2.00
Tumbler - small footed.	3.00
Tumbler - large footed	3.50
Wine bottle/stopper	22.00

Scroll

SCROLL (Comet) --U.S. Glass Co.

	Green
Creamer	2.50
Cup	1.50
Saucer	.75
Plate	2.50
Sugar	2.50

SHARON (Cabbage Rose)---Federal Glass Co. (1935-39)

Pink, Yellow, Green, Clear

Bowl - fruit	7.25
Bowl - oval vegetable	6.00
Bowl - 8½"	5.25
Bowl - soup	2.75
Bowl - cereal.	2.75
Bowl - nappy	2.50
Bowl - 5"	2.75
Butter Dish/cover	20.00
Cake Plate - footed	10.50
Candy Jar/cover	14.00
Cheese Dish/cover	22.00
Creamer	4.50
Cup	3.25
Saucer	2.00
Pitcher - with or without lip	23.00
Plate - dinner	3.50
Plate - luncheon	2.50
Plate - pie	2.25
Platter	6.50
Salt and Pepper	9.00

Sharon

Sherbet 2.50
Sugar/cover 5.75
Tumbler - 4"............................... 3.50
Tumbler - 5"............................... 4.25
Tumbler - footed 6.00

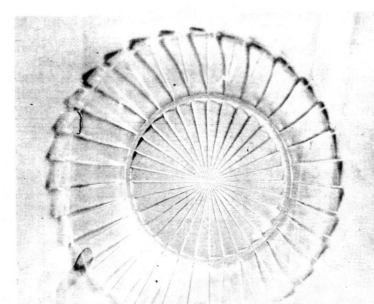

Sierra

SIERRA (Pinwheel)-----Jeannette Glass Co. (1931-32)

Pink, Green

Bowl - oval vegetable	5.50
Bowl - deep	8.00
Bowl - nappy	2.25
Bowl - soup	2.50
Butter Dish/cover	17.50
Creamer	3.25
Cup	3.25
Saucer	1.75
Pitcher	14.50
Plate - 10"	5.00
Plate - 9"	3.50
Plate - 6"	2.25
Platter	6.00
Salt and Pepper	8.25
Sherbet	2.75
Sugar /cover	3.75
Tray - handled	5.25

SPIRAL-----Hocking Glass Co. (1928-29)

	Green
Bowl - 8"	4.50
Bowl - 7"	4.50
Bowl - 5"	2.00
Bowl - Ice	4.50
Creamer	3.25
Cup	2.50
Saucer	1.25
Pitcher	8.00
Pitcher - syrup	6.50
Plate - 8"	2.50
Plate - 6"	1.50
Sandwich plate - handle in center	7.50
Sherbet	2.00
Sugar	3.50
Tumbler	2.50

Spiral

SPORTSMAN SERIES-----Hazel Atlas Glass Co.

	Cobalt Blue
Ice Bowl	6.00
Pitcher - sailboat	10.00
Plate - sailboat	3.50
Shaker - dogs & horses	12.00
Shaker - dogs & horses - sailboats	20.00
Shaker/lid/strainer - windmill	20.00
Tumblers - sailboat	3.00 to 5.00
Tumbler - golf H/A mark on bottom	6.50

Sportsman Series

STARLIGHT

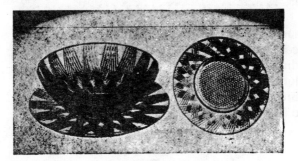

STARLIGHT-----Hazel Atlas (1938)

Pink, Clear, Cobalt blue, Monax

Bowl - 8" handled 10.00

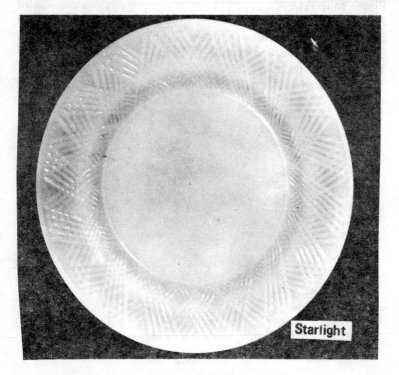

Starlight

Bowl - 11½"..................................	5.00
Bowl - 8½"...................................	3.25
Bowl - 5½"...................................	2.00
Creamer	2.75
Cup	2.75
Saucer	1.50
Plate - cake.................................	4.50
Plate - dinner	3.00
Plate - luncheon	2.50
Plate - bread and butter	2.00
Salt and Pepper	7.50
Sugar	3.00

STRAWBERRY------Origin Unknown

Green, Pink, Crystal

Bowl - deep 7½".............................	7.50
Bowl - deep 6½".............................	4.75
Bowl - 4"......	2.50
Butter Dish/cover...........................	20.00
Compote	5.75
Creamer	4.25
Pickle Dish-oval shaped......................	5.75
Pickle Dish - handled	4.50
Plate - 7½".................................	3.25
Plate - 6"	2.75
Sherbet....................................	3.25
Sugar - cover..............................	5.25
Tumbler...................................	5.00

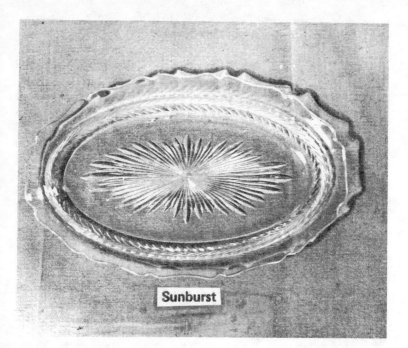

Sunburst

SUNBURST-----Jeannette Glass Co.

Crystal

Bowl - nappy	1.50
Bowl - serving	2.50
Creamer	2.75
Cup	2.00
Saucer	1.25
Plate - dinner	2.75
Plate - 12" sandwich	3.25
Plate - 12" cake	3.25
Plate - salad	2.00
Relish Dish - divided	2.25
Sugar	3.00
Tumbler	3.00

SUNFLOWER-----Origin Unknown

Pink, Green

Ash Tray	2.25
Bowl - 8" oval	5.50
Bowl - 5" serving	2.75
Bowl - cereal	2.50
Cake Plate - footed	8.00
Creamer	4.25
Cup	3.25
Saucer	1.75
Plate - 9"	3.50
Plate - luncheon	3.00
Plate - pie	2.00
Platter	6.00
Sherbet	2.50
Sugar	3.25
Tumbler - footed	5.00

Sunflower

Swirl

SWIRL (Petal Swirl)-----Jeannette Glass Co. (1937-38)

Teal Blue, Pink, Delfite

Ash Tray	2.50
Bowl - console, footed	12.00
Bowl - 10" fruit,/handles/footed	12.00
Bowl - 9"	7.50
Bowl - 5"	5.00
Bowl - lugs	2.75
Butter Dish/cover	22.00
Candlesticks (green-rare)	11.00
Candy Dish/cover	12.00
Candy Dish - 3 legged	5.75
Coaster	1.50
Creamer (some have enameled flowers)	5.50
Cup	3.75
Saucer	2.00
Plate - cake	9.00
Plate - dinner	3.75
Plate - salad	3.25
Plate - bread and butter	2.50
Platter	6.50
Salt and Pepper	9.00

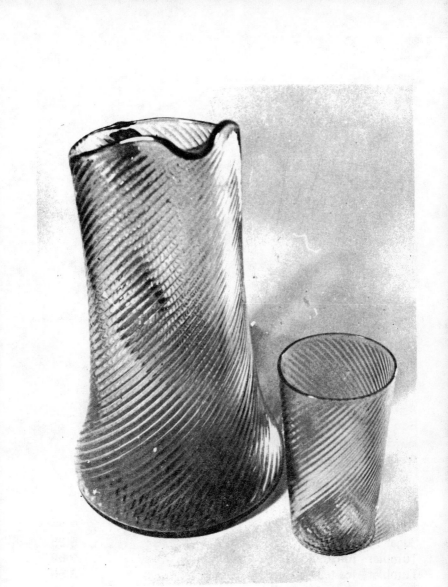

SWIRL

	Green
Pitcher	20.00
Tumbler	5.00

Swirl

Sherbet, footed 2.25
Sugar 5.25
Tumbler - juice................................ 3.00
Tumbler - ice tea 3.50
Tumbler - ice tea footed...................... 4.00
Vase - 2 styles 8.50

TEA ROOM-----Indiana Glass Co. (1927-31)

Pink, Green, Clear

Bowl - oval vegetable	5.50
Bowl - deep fruit	5.75
Bowl - footed, oblong.	3.50
Bowl - 8"	4.50
Bowl - finger.	2.50
Candlesticks	8.00
Creamer	3.50
Cup	3.25
Saucer	2.00
Goblet	3.50
Ice Bucket	9.00
Lamp - electric	8.00
Mustard Dish/cover	6.00
Parfait	3.50
Pitcher	10.00
Plate - dinner	3.25
Plate - luncheon	2.75
Plate - salad	2.50

Tea Room

Relish - 2 part	5.00
Salt and Pepper	8.75
Sandwich Plate/handle in center	8.50
Sherbet	3.25
Sugar/cover	5.00
Sugar and Creamer on tray/handle in center	8.50
Tumbler - large	3.50
Tumbler - ice tea	2.75
Tumbler - water	2.50
Tumbler - juice	2.25
Vase	9.00

**Texas Centennial Glasses
1936**

1936 Texas Centennial Glass .... 5.00 ea.

THISTLE-----MacBeth-Evans Glass Co.

Pink, Green

Bowl - vegetable	6.50
Bowl - fruit	5.75
Bowl - cereal	2.50
Creamer	3.25
Cup	3.00
Saucer	1.75
Plate - grill	3.50
Plate - dinner	3.25
Plate - luncheon	2.75
Plate - bread & butter	2.00
Sherbet - footed	2.75
Sugar	3.50

THUMBPRINT (Pear Optic)-----Federal Glass Co. (1929)

	Green
Bowl - nappy	4.50
Bowl - cereal	2.75
Creamer	3.00
Cup	2.50
Saucer	1.25
Plate - dinner	2.75
Plate - luncheon	2.25
Plate - sherbet	1.50
Salt and Pepper	7.50
Sherbet	2.50
Sugar	2.75
Tumbler	2.50

Thumbprint

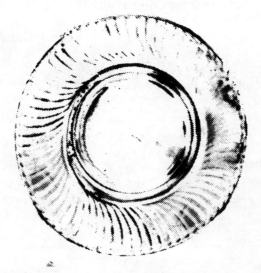

TWISTED OPTIC-----Imperial Glass Company

Green, Amber, Pink

Bowl - console	6.00
Bowl - vegetable	4.50
Bowl - nappy	2.50
Candlesticks	9.00
Candy Dish/cover	10.00
Coaster	2.00
Creamer	3.50
Cup	3.50
Saucer	1.75
Pitcher	9.00
Plate - luncheon	2.75
Plate - salad	2.25
Plate - sherbet	2.00
Sherbet	2.00
Sugar	3.00
Tumbler	3.50

VERNON-----Indiana Glass Company (1931)

Yellow, Green, Clear

Bowl - cereal	2.00
Bowl - vegetable	3.75
Creamer	3.25
Cup	3.00
Saucer	1.50
Plate - 11"	4.25
Plate - luncheon	3.00
Plate - pie	2.00
Relish Dish	5.75
Sherbet	2.25
Sugar	3.50
Tumbler - footed	4.00

Virginian

VIRGINIAN

Pink, Green

Plate 3.50

VITROCK-----Hocking Glass

Bowl - serving 4.00
Bowl - cereal 3.25
Bowl - soup 3.00
Bowl - berry 2.50
Creamer 3.00
Cup 2.50
      Saucer 1.00
Plate - dinner 2.75
Plate - luncheon 2.50
Plate - dessert 2.00
Plate - bread & butter 1.75
Platter 3.50
Sugar 3.25

WATERFORD (Waffle) - Anchor Hocking Co. (1938-44)

Pink, Clear

Ash Tray	2.00
Bowl - vegetable	5.00
Bowl - nappy	2.75

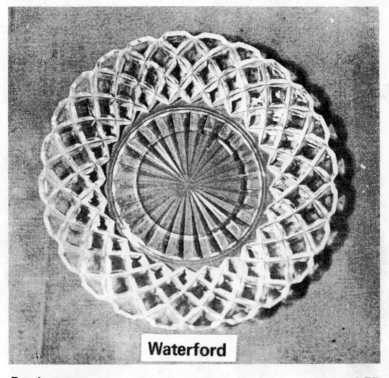

Waterford

Bowl - soup	1.75
Butter Dish/cover	17.50
Coaster	1.75
Creamer	3.25
Cup	3.00
Saucer	2.00
Goblet (Clear)	3.00
Lazy Susan	8.75
Pitcher - 2 sizes	8.00-11.00
Plate - sandwich	5.75
Plate - cake	4.50

Plate - dinner	3.50
Plate - salad	2.00
Plate - dessert	1.75
Salt and Pepper (Clear)	5.00
Sherbet	2.00
Sugar	3.25
Tumbler - footed	3.00

WINDOWPANE-----Hazel Atlas Co.

Green, Clear

Candy Jar/lid	12.00
Creamer	3.50
Sherbet	2.25
Sugar	3.50

Windowpane

WINDSOR----Jeannette Glass Co. (1936-40)

Pink, Green, Clear

Ash Tray	2.00
Bowl - console	8.50
Bowl - handled - round	6.75
Bowl - oval vegetable	5.50
Bowl - serving	5.50
Bowl - serving - eye-shaped	9.00
Bowl - 3-legged	4.00
Bowl - soup	2.50

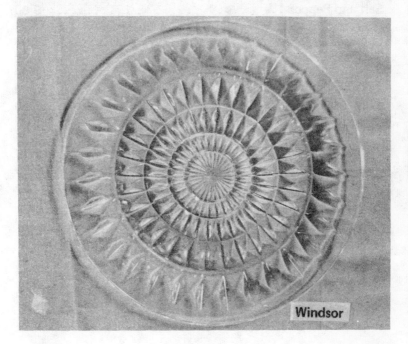

Windsor

Bowl - cereal	2.25
Bowl - berry	2.00
Butter Dish/cover	20.00
Candlesticks	10.75
Candy Jar/cover	9.50
Coaster	2.00
Creamer	3.25

145

Cup 3.00
      Saucer 2.00
Pitcher - small 8.50
Pitcher - large 13.50
Plate - 14″. 6.25
Plate - cake 7.00
Plate - 9″ dinner. 3.50
Plate - salad 2.50
Plate - dessert. 2.00
Platter 6.50
Powder Dish/cover. 6.50
Relish Tray with 4 bowls 6.00
Salt and Pepper 9.00
Sherbet 2.50
Sugar/cover 5.00
Tray - 14″ handled. 6.50
Tray - 16″. 8.00
Tray - square - large 5.00
Tray - square - small 2.50
Tray - oblong. 3.50
Tumbler - 3″. 2.25
Tumbler - 4″. 2.75
Tumbler - 5″. 3.25
Tumbler - footed 3.25

PEANUT BUTTER

Cup & Saucer Set 4.00

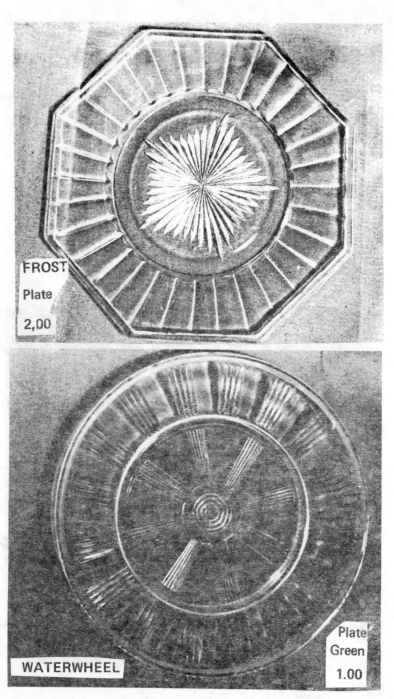

FROST
Plate
2.00

WATERWHEEL

Plate
Green
1.00

148

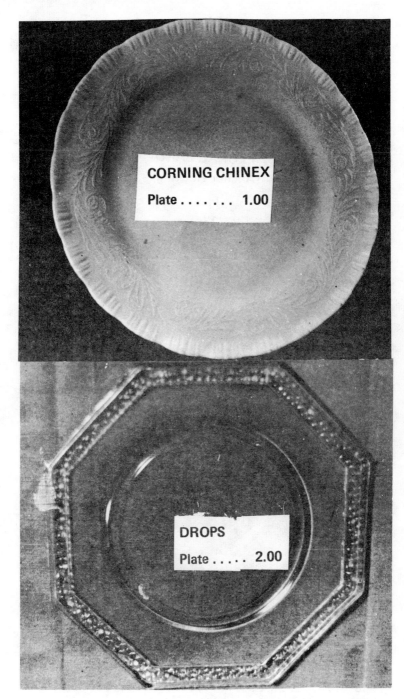

CORNING CHINEX

Plate 1.00

DROPS

Plate 2.00

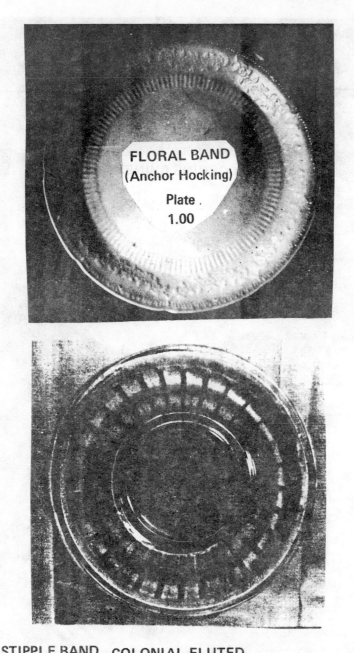

FLORAL BAND
(Anchor Hocking)
Plate
1.00

STIPPLE BAND - COLONIAL FLUTED

	Pink
Plate	1.00

BLOCK -

Cordial Glass

Green/Platinum Rim

. . . . 6.00

DOLPHIN-----Several Glass Co. produced this

Green, Pink, Clear

Bowl. 8.00
Candleholders - small 11.00
Candleholders - large 22.00
Large Fish Boat 7.50

Refrigerator dish set

..... 2.50

Amber

Mixing Bowl Set 6.00

Sure Shot Glass - Green/Aluminum 7.50

Refrigerator dish with cobalt lid 5.00

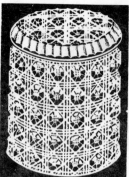

Condensed Milk Jar/top
4½" high, 3" diameter in pressed crystal 30.00

Condensed Milk Jar
5¾" high, 2¾" diameter
Clear crystal, colonial panel with glass top 30.00

Covered Honey Dish 5½" square, footed,
Crystal deep cut floral and diamond pattern 5.00

154

Frosted Red Band
  Beverage set - 8 glasses & pitcher 15.00

Optic Grape
  Beverage set - 8 glasses & pitcher 15.00

3-Pc.

Sets

7 In. Plates

Feeding Dishes

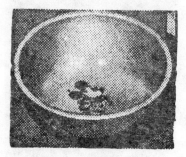

Cereal Bowls

Drinking Mugs

Mickey Mouse Childrens Set

Green, Coral

Bowl, Drinking Mug, Feeding Dish, Plate 30.00

Ovenware "Glasbake" /Chromium Finish
Frame

Crystal

1½ qt. Oval Baker.............................. 4.50
9" Pie plate 4.00
1½ qt. round baker 4.50
1 qt. casseroles - covered 5.00
Utility Dish - rectangle......................... 5.00

Plain Crystal Syrup Pitcher. 20.00
Fluted Crystal Syrup Pitcher 25.00

CRYSTAL
SHELF
SUPPORTS

1-PC. SUPPORT   2-PC. SUPPORT

Crystal Shelf Supports . . . . .10.00 ea.

Graduated Heavy Crystal Dipper
    13″ long, black enameled wood handle 15.00

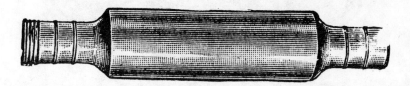

Crystal Rolling Pin
    16″, one piece, open end, can be filled with cracked
    ice or cold water to prevent dough sticking. 10.00

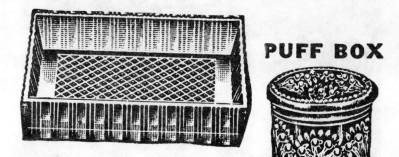

PUFF BOX

Puff Box
    3½″ diameter, orange blossom, royal and
    golden blending 15.00

Crystal Candy Tray
    7¼″ x 5¼″ jewel cut bottoms, prism side. 15.00

Covered crystal glass jars 4¾" high
   on white enameled revolving tray............ 25.00

ACTUAL PHOTOGRAPH

Crystal Jars/aluminum tops on white
   enameled revolving tray 20.00

Kitchen Set

	Green
Bowl - 9½″ rolled edge mixing	3.00
Bowl - 7½″ rolled edge mixing	2.50
Butter Dish & cover	5.00
Drippings bowl	2.00
Measuring cup	2.50
Reamer	2.25
Refrigerator jar/cover	3.00
Salt and Pepper	3.50

4 Piece Range Set - Milk glass/green lettering
    aluminum top
    Salt, pepper, flour, sugar 5.00

3 Piece Range Set - Milk glass/aluminum tops
    Salt, pepper, drippings dish 4.50

Round Covered Bean Pot - clear 25.00

Toothpick and Match Holders . . . . 10.00 ea.

Crystal, bright tin caps.

Jelly Molds & Glasses, crystal . . . . 2.50 ea.

Milk Glass/metal tops - Salt & Peppers . . . . 4.00 ea
Clear/metal tops - Salt & Peppers . . . . 2.00 ea
Clear - Reamer 3.00
Black Amethyst - Reamer. .150.00

Milk Glass Sunkist Reamer 5.00

Index

OTHER HIGHLY RECOMMENDED BOOKS & PERIODICALS

The Depression Glass Dictionary, by Glenita Stearns, Box 11331, Tacoma, Wash. 98411

Depression Glass In Color by Sandra McPhee Stout, 661 Dodson Road, Ephrata, Wash. 98823

Colored Glassware of the Depression Era by Hazel Marie Weatherman, 4501 Jackson Dr., Rt. 12, Springfield, Mo. 65804

Depression Glass Daze, Box 57, Otisville, Mich. 48463

Glassware Gazette, Box 377, Bettendorf, Iowa 52722

Antiques Journal, Box 467, Kewanee, Ill. 61443

Antique News, Box B, Marietta, Pa. 17547

Antique Trader, Box 1050, Dubuque, Iowa 52001

Coins, Box 274, Iola, Wisc. 54945

The Collectibles, P.O. Box 105, Newton, N.C. 28658

Collectors News, Box 156, Grundy Center, Iowa 50638

Collectors Weekly, Box 1119, Kermit, Texas 79745

Collectors World, Box 217, Conroe, Texas 77301

Early American Life, 1001 Bevridge Road, Richmond, Va. 23226

Eastern Antiquity, 1 Dogwood Drive, Washington, N.J. 07882

Gems and Minerals, Box 687, Mentone, Calif. 92359

Good Ole Days, Box 412, Danver, Mass. 01923

Hobbies, 1006 S. Michigan Ave., Chicago, Ill. 60605

Mid-Atlantic Antique Journal, Box 2092, Falls Church, Ca. 22042

National Bottle Gazette, Box 136, Amador City, Calif., 95601

Numismatic News, Iola, Wisc. 54945

Old Bottle Magazine, Box 243, Bend, Oregon 97701

Relics, Box 3668, Austin, Texas 78704

Spinning Wheel, Box 286, Hanover, Pa. 17331

Stamps, 153 Waverly Place, New York, N.Y. 10014

Tri-State Trader, Box 90, Knightstown, Ind. 46148

Western Antique Mart, Box 2171, Eugene, Oregon 97402

Western Treasures, 6660 Reseda Blvd., Reseda, Calif. 71335

Western Collector, 511 Harrison St., San Francisco, Calif. 94105

********ACKNOWLEDGEMENT********

The bulk of the photos in this book were taken by Joe A. Gibson of the fabulous 12,000 piece .... collection of depression glass owned by Phil   and Carolyn Moran of San Antonio, Texas.

These are mighty nice folks, so drop by or call sometime at ....

PHIL MORAN INTERIORS
Member
AMERICAN SOCIETY OF APPRAISERS
Appraisals of Antiques, Fine Arts and
Estates for Insurance, Taxes and Resale.
Liquidations and Auctions

512/734-5668

203 W. Mistletoe   San Antonio, Tex. 78212